TRIBUTARIES OF THE CHESAPEAKE BAY

By Heather Moore Niver

Gareth Stevens
Publishing

Please visit our website, www.garethstevens.com. For a free color catalog of all our high-quality books, call toll free 1-800-542-2595 or fax 1-877-542-2596.

Library of Congress Cataloging-in-Publication Data

Niver, Heather Moore.
Tributaries of the Chesapeake Bay / by Heather Moore Niver.
  p. cm. — (Exploring the Chesapeake Bay)
Includes index.
ISBN 978-1-4339-9793-8 (pbk.)
ISBN 978-1-4339-9794-5 (6-pack)
ISBN 978-1-4339-9792-1 (library binding)
1. Chesapeake Bay (Md. and Va.) — Juvenile literature. 2. Estuarine ecology — Juvenile literature. 3. Estuarine ecology — Chesapeake Bay (Md. and Va.). I. Niver, Heather Moore. II. Title.
QH95.9 N58 2014
577.7'86—d23

First Edition

Published in 2014 by
Gareth Stevens Publishing
111 East 14th Street, Suite 349
New York, NY 10003

Designer: Michael Flynn and Katelyn E. Reynolds
Editor: Kristen Rajczak

Photo credits: Cover, p. 1 Cameron Davidson/Stone/Getty Images; pp. 4, 5 iStockphoto/Thinkstock.com; pp. 7, 8–9, 14, 17 (maps), 18 (Susquehanna, Potomac, Rappahannock), 19, 20, 21, 26, 27, 28, 29 courtesy of the Integration and Application Network, University of Maryland Center for Environmental Science; p. 8 PHOTO 24/Brand X Pictures/Getty Images; pp. 10–11 MPI/Getty Images; p. 13 Edwin Remsberg/Taxi/Getty Images; p. 15 NASA/JPL; pp. 16–17 Roberto A. Sanchez/E+/Getty Images; p. 18 (York) Zorin09/Wikipedia.com; p. 18 (James) Thea Ganoe/Wikipedia.com; p. 23 Peter Essick/Aurora/Getty Images; pp. 24–25 Paul Souders/Photodisc/Getty Images.

Printed in the United States of America

CPSIA compliance information: Batch #CS13GS: For further information contact Gareth Stevens, New York, New York at 1-800-542-2595.

CONTENTS

The Great Shellfish Bay 4

Shelter, Cleaning, and Protection. 8

Trickle Down: Tributaries 10

People and Places. 12

When Salt Meets Fresh 16

Major Tributaries 18

In and Around the Bay. 20

Watershed Wellness 22

The Habitat Needs Help!. 26

Chesapeake Conservation. 28

Glossary. 30

For More Information. 31

Index 32

Words in the glossary appear in **bold** type the
first time they are used in the text.

THE GREAT SHELLFISH BAY

About 12,000 years ago, glaciers melted and flooded an area of the eastern United States now called the Susquehanna River valley. This enormous flood also created the mighty Chesapeake Bay. A bay is a body of water that is partly surrounded by land.

More than 17 million people and 3,600 species of plants and animals call the Chesapeake Bay home. Hundreds of species of fish swim through its waters at some point in their lives. The bay's name comes from the Algonquian word *chesepiooc*, which many believe means "great shellfish bay."

BLUE CRAB

BEHOLD THE "HOLE"

In spite of its size, most of the Chesapeake Bay isn't deep. The average depth, including all its **tributaries**, is only around 21 feet (6 m). Someone who is 6 feet (1.8 m) tall could walk through more than 700,000 acres (283,500 ha) of the bay without getting their hat wet! The deepest part is 174 feet (53 m). Located south of Annapolis, Maryland, this spot is known as the "hole."

People have lived around the Chesapeake Bay for thousands of years!

The Chesapeake Bay is the biggest estuary in the United States. An estuary is an area on the coast where a river meets the sea. In the Chesapeake Bay, the freshwater from tributaries mixes with salt water from the Atlantic Ocean. The bay has more fish and shellfish than any other estuary in the country.

WHAT'S A WATERSHED?

To picture a watershed, imagine a small stream that trickles into a river. The river runs into a lake. Everything around the stream, river, and lake is part of one watershed, because all the water in that area flows into the same lake. One watershed is separated from another by high points like hills or slopes.

Water flows over, under, or through land on its way to a stream, river, or lake. This is called a watershed (also known as a basin or drainage basin). Your local creek or stream is a small watershed. The Chesapeake Bay has the third-largest watershed in the world. The bay's watershed covers 64,000 square miles (165,760 sq km).

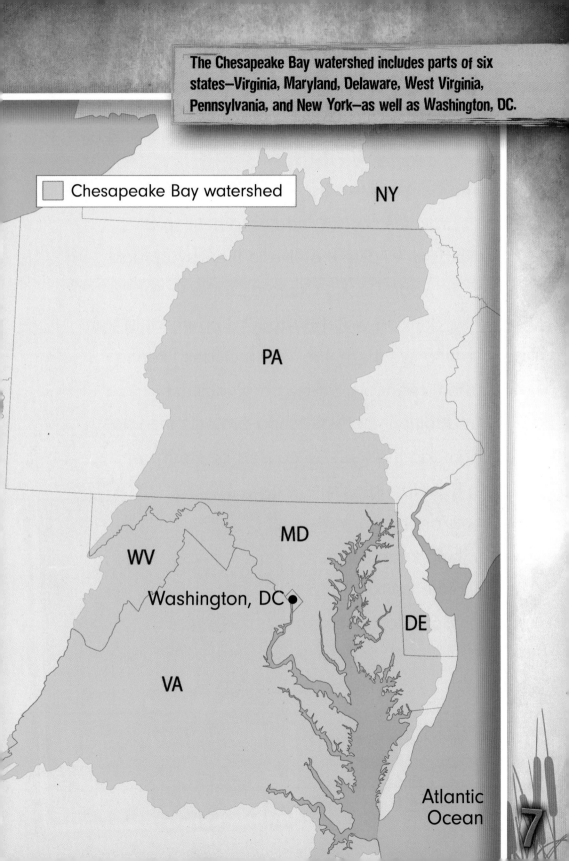

The Chesapeake Bay watershed includes parts of six states—Virginia, Maryland, Delaware, West Virginia, Pennsylvania, and New York—as well as Washington, DC.

☐ Chesapeake Bay watershed

NY

PA

MD

WV

Washington, DC●

DE

VA

Atlantic
Ocean

SHELTER, CLEANING, AND PROTECTION

The Chesapeake Bay has many important roles. It provides shelter, food, and nesting for many kinds of wildlife that live in the bay at least part of the year. Through its forests, the watershed filters the drinking water of about 75 percent of the people who live there, too. This includes filtering waste from residents, farms, and industries.

In addition, the watershed protects the coast from damage that can be caused by storms and waves. Riparian forests, or forests on the bank of a river, help keep soil in place so the banks of the streams don't collapse.

The bald eagle is just one kind of bird that makes its home in the bay watershed.

FEATHERS, FINS, AND MORE

All kinds of wildlife can be found near the Chesapeake Bay! Birds like ducks, swans, and geese come back to the area each fall. Hundreds of other kinds of birds pass through during **migration**. Bald eagles depend on the Chesapeake Bay as a safe place to build their nests. Striped bass, eel, bobcats, and blue crabs are just a few more bay residents.

The health of the Chesapeake Bay has a great impact on the plants and animals that live there.

TRICKLE DOWN: TRIBUTARIES

Streams, creeks, and rivers that flow into larger bodies of water are called tributaries. The Chesapeake Bay includes more than 100,000 tributaries in its watershed. The five major tributary systems for the bay are the Potomac, the Susquehanna, the Rappahannock, the York, and the James Rivers. Together, these five rivers provide about 90 percent of the bay's freshwater.

The Susquehanna River is one of the longest rivers in the eastern United States at about 455 miles (732 km). This river system alone provides the bay with more than half its freshwater. Other significant tributaries of Chesapeake Bay include the Patapsco, the Chester, the Choptank, the Patuxent, the Nanticoke, and the Pocomoke Rivers.

BIG BAY, BIG NUMBERS

The Chesapeake watershed has 11,684 miles (18,800 km) of shoreline, if you include islands and wetlands such as swamps. That means it has more shoreline than the entire West Coast of the United States! Tributaries pump more than 51 billion gallons (193 billion l) of water into the bay every day. And almost a million waterfowl spend their winters on the bay.

The first permanent English settlement in North America was Jamestown, Virginia, founded right on the James River!

PEOPLE AND PLACES

Many major cities are found in the Chesapeake Bay watershed and along its tributaries, including Washington, DC, and Baltimore, Maryland. More and more people relocate to the Chesapeake watershed every year. Between 2000 and 2005, the watershed's population grew by 170,000 a year—that's 466 people every day!

Tourism has become important to the Chesapeake Bay economy as fishing, boating, birding, and hunting in and along the bay and its tributaries are common. Since the earliest settlers arrived, commercial fishing has been a significant bay industry, too. Two of the East Coast's biggest ports, Baltimore and Hampton Roads, Virginia, are both on the bay.

TRIBUTARY CITIES

While there are many cities on the Chesapeake Bay, there are even more on its tributaries! Both Newport News and Richmond, Virginia, are on the James River. The Rappahannock River flows right past Fredericksburg, Virginia. And the Potomac River is an important geographic feature of Washington, DC!

Blue crab, rockfish, **menhaden**, and eastern oysters provide billions of dollars for fishing businesses.

13

In 1706, Baltimore Harbor started out as a location for tobacco shipping. Baltimore was officially founded in 1729. The Port of Baltimore became one of the country's leaders in shipbuilding. Located on the Patapsco River, Baltimore has been a leader in oyster canning and steelwork, too.

Hampton Roads is one of the southernmost areas of the Chesapeake watershed. Also called Tidewater, the Elizabeth and the James Rivers flow through it. Fishing is popular here, both for business and for fun. It's the largest area of military and government facilities in the world. Almost one-quarter of our country's active military workers are stationed in Hampton Roads.

TRAVELING THE SUSQUEHANNA

The Susquehanna River starts its journey to the bay up north in Cooperstown, New York. Cooperstown sits at the foot of Otsego Lake, which provides about 60 percent of the water the Susquehanna brings to the Chesapeake Bay. This area of the watershed is covered with forests and farms.

James River

Elizabeth
River

About 1.6 million people live in Hampton Roads, shown here.
The area includes Virginia Beach and Newport News, Virginia,
among other cities and towns.

15

WHEN SALT MEETS FRESH

In general, the waters in the lower parts of the Chesapeake Bay are salty. Freshwater tends to be found at the head of the bay. In between, the water is a mix of freshwater and salt water, which is called brackish water. Most of the bay's water is brackish.

Every spring, snowmelt and rainfall cause the bay's tributaries to rise, and freshwater rushes to the bay, pushing back the salt water. After the dry summer, autumn water levels are much lower. Salt water makes up a much greater percentage of the estuary waters then.

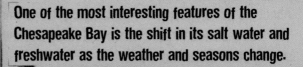

One of the most interesting features of the Chesapeake Bay is the shift in its salt water and freshwater as the weather and seasons change.

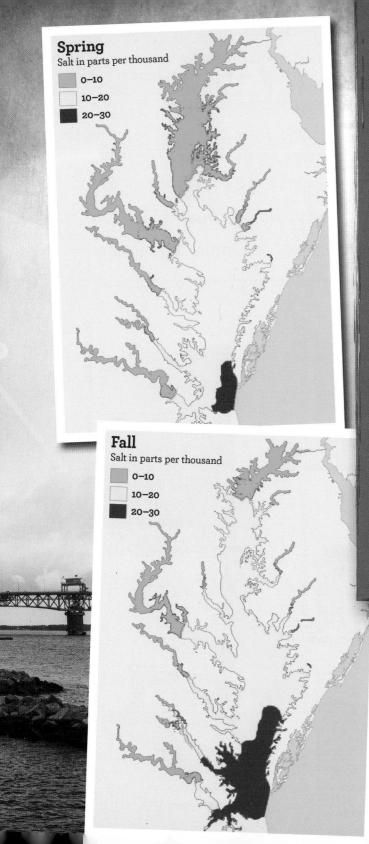

Spring
Salt in parts per thousand

- 0–10
- 10–20
- 20–30

Fall
Salt in parts per thousand

- 0–10
- 10–20
- 20–30

YORK RIVER

The York River flows for more than 30 miles (48 km) in eastern Virginia, emptying into the western part of the Chesapeake Bay. Its marshes and other **habitats**, as well as the wildlife that lives there, are protected by the bounds of York River State Park and the Chesapeake Bay National Estuarine Research Reserve. While keeping the river's ecosystem healthy has been a priority, visitors can still enjoy its hiking trails and fishing spots.

MAJOR TRIBUTARIES

Since the bay and its tributaries can provide food, water, and transportation, it's no wonder so many communities have grown up around them! Use this map to find some of the major tributaries of the Chesapeake Bay.

SUSQUEHANNA RIVER

POTOMAC RIVER

RAPPAHANNOCK RIVER

JAMES RIVER

YORK RIVER

NY

PA

SUSQUEHANNA RIVER

PATAPSCO RIVER

MD

WV

PATUXENT RIVER

CHOPTANK RIVER

Washington, DC

DE

POTOMAC RIVER

RAPPAHANNOCK RIVER

VA

YORK RIVER

Atlantic
Ocean

JAMES RIVER

19

IN AND AROUND THE BAY

An ecosystem is all the living things in an area. They all depend on one another in some way. Water, soil, and sunlight all play a role in an ecosystem, too. The Chesapeake Bay's watershed is one example of a large ecosystem. It includes the bay, its tributaries, and all the plants, animals, and people it supports.

The Chesapeake watershed provides a wide variety of habitats for its plants and animals. Forests, wetlands, rivers, and the bay itself are all home to animals such as horseshoe crabs, pumpkinseed fish, and green sea turtles, among others. Forests make up 58 percent of the Chesapeake's watershed.

Industry in the watershed can produce pollution that affects the bay's ecosystem.

WILDLIFE IN WILD WATERS

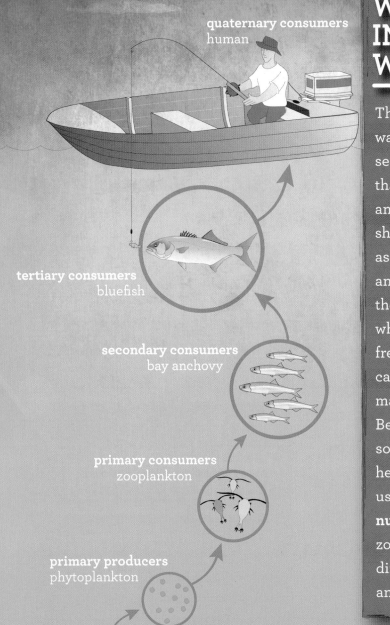

quaternary consumers
human

tertiary consumers
bluefish

secondary consumers
bay anchovy

primary consumers
zooplankton

primary producers
phytoplankton

The movement of the waters during each season does more than shift salt water and freshwater. It shifts materials such as **plankton**, oxygen, and **larvae** through the bay. The area where salt water and freshwater mix is called the "zone of maximum turbidity." Because there are so many **nutrients** here, many animals use this area as their **nursery**. Without this zone, it might be more difficult for these animals to reproduce.

Food chains and webs are a major part of the Chesapeake Bay ecosystem. If links in a food chain disappear because of pollution or overfishing, the whole ecosystem can be affected.

WATERSHED WELLNESS

The important waterways of the Chesapeake Bay have suffered over the years. The growth, or bloom, of algae in the bay has blocked out sunlight and removed oxygen from the water. This creates areas called "dead zones" where it's difficult or impossible for underwater grasses and animals to live in the bay.

Farms surrounding the bay and its tributaries put a lot of pollutants and soil into the water. Wastewater treatment plants are another common way pollution ends up in the bay. Old industrial and power plants often send harmful materials into the air, too. Today, many industries are upgrading their facilities to reduce their impact.

PEOPLE AND POLLUTION IN THE ECOSYSTEM

People are naturally a part of the Chesapeake's ecosystem, but they could have an effect on it as well. **Runoff** from gardens can carry harmful materials into the bay and tributaries. Gases from our cars and buses pollute the air, too. Even something as small as not cleaning up your dog's waste can eventually be damaging to the bay, if it's washed into the water.

Fuel from a boat leaked into the bay here.
What harm could it have caused?

23

As more people choose to live along the Chesapeake Bay and its tributaries, cities become more crowded. So, people move outside the city and build houses in areas known as suburbs. This is called urban sprawl. It takes land from forests, wetlands, and well-managed farms.

Naturally, more people means more fishing. The bay and its tributaries have always been full of fish and shellfish. Because of overfishing and water pollution, however, there are lower numbers and fewer kinds of fish swimming through the bay today. River herring, Atlantic menhaden, blue crabs, oysters, and striped bass (rockfish) all struggle to survive.

As the population in the watershed has grown to more than 17 million people, fish populations have continued to decrease.

PAVEMENT POLLUTION

More people and houses mean that more roads, highways, and parking lots are covering the ground with hard surfaces like pavement. Instead of slowly being absorbed into the ground, water rushes over **impervious** surfaces, such as sidewalks and streets, into streams and rivers and storm sewers. The extra water causes **erosion** and flooding.

THE HABITAT NEEDS HELP!

As temperature cycles change around the world, the Chesapeake Bay ecosystem is dealing with the effects of a changing climate. Higher water temperatures put stress on fish that live in cold waters, such as brook trout. Some grasses like eelgrass can't grow if the water temperature is too high.

These changes in weather seem to be causing bigger, more frequent storms that raise concern about water levels, too. In the twentieth century, sea levels rose by 1 foot (0.3 m). Scientists think that waters could rise 17 to 28 inches (43 to 71 cm) above 1990s levels by the year 2095. Thousands of miles of shoreline could be lost.

FLOODED MARSH AFTER A STORM

TRIBUTARIES IN TROUBLE, TOO?

Groups like the Chesapeake Bay Foundation (CBF) are certainly concerned with the Chesapeake Bay itself. The CBF and other groups work together to keep the tributaries healthy as well. In July 2012, representatives from Pennsylvania, Virginia, Maryland, and Washington, DC, met with the Chesapeake Bay Commission and the Environmental Protection Agency to report their efforts to reduce pollution and restore water quality in their part of the watershed.

Extremely high temperatures in 2005 killed off a great deal of eelgrass in the lower Chesapeake. It will take years for the area to recover, but studies of bay tributaries suggest new grass might be grown from seed.

CHESAPEAKE CONSERVATION

In 2012, a report on the bay's health revealed that it's improving. Farming and other kinds of agriculture are a big source of the problem, but they're also one of the best ways to get the bay back in shape. The CBF works with farmers to put up fencing to keep livestock and other animals out of streams. They also plant and care for sections of forest and grass around the farms.

Efforts to help bay animals are being made, too. The Maryland Oyster Gardening Program makes it easy for residents to help "grow" new oysters right along their own docks.

WATER QUALITY TESTING IN THE PATUXENT RIVER

OYSTER GARDENING

In oyster gardens, oysters are grown in cages made from wire mesh. The cages hang from docks. Several thousand seed oysters grow in the cage for a year, until they're about 2 inches (5 cm) long. The grown oysters are returned to CBF and replanted on a reef where no harvesting is allowed. There, the oysters can continue to grow.

Oysters play a major role in filtering bay water, but they're still rebounding from the years of disease and overfishing that have decreased their population.

GLOSSARY

erosion: the process of wearing away by wind, water, or glacial ice

habitat: the natural place where an animal or plant lives

impervious: not allowing entrance

larvae: bugs in an early life stage that have a wormlike form

menhaden: a fish from the herring family that lives along the East Coast and is often fished for bait, oil, or fertilizer

migration: the act of moving from one place to another in order to find food or have babies

nursery: a place or natural surroundings that support breeding and development

nutrient: something a living thing needs to grow and stay alive

plankton: a tiny plant or animal that floats in the ocean

runoff: the rain or other precipitation that flows over land into a river or stream, usually carrying with it waste, soil, or other materials

tourism: the business of drawing in tourists, or people traveling to visit another place

tributary: a stream or river flowing into a larger body of water

FOR MORE INFORMATION

Books

Johnson, Rebecca L. *A Journey into an Estuary.* Minneapolis, MN: Carolrhoda Books, 2004.

Jones, Rebecca C. *Captain John Smith's Big and Beautiful Bay.* Atglen, PA: Schiffer Publishing, Ltd., 2011.

Rice, William B. *Chesapeake Bay Wetlands.* Westminster, CA: Teacher Created Materials, 2005.

Websites

Chesapeake Bay Watershed Geography and Facts
www.cbf.org/about-the-bay/more-than-just-the-bay/
chesapeake-bay-watershed-geography-and-facts
Find out more about the Chesapeake Bay and its huge watershed.

Streams & Rivers
www.chesapeakebay.net/fieldguide/categories/category/
streams_rivers
Read facts and watch videos about common plants and animals that hang out in the Chesapeake's plentiful tributaries.

INDEX

brackish water 16

Chesapeake Bay Foundation (CBF) 27, 28, 29

Choptank River 10, 18

cities 12, 14, 15, 24

dead zones 22

ecosystem 17, 20, 21, 22

erosion 25

farms 8, 14, 22, 24, 28

fish 4, 6, 24, 26

food 8, 18

food chains 21

forests 8, 14, 20, 24, 28

freshwater 6, 10, 16, 21

habitats 17, 20

industries 8, 12, 13, 14, 20, 22

James River 10, 11, 12, 14, 18

nesting 8, 9

overfishing 21, 24, 29

oyster gardens 28, 29

Patapsco River 10, 14

Patuxent River 10, 28

people 4, 5, 12, 15, 20, 22, 24, 25

pollution 20, 21, 22, 24, 27

Potomac River 10, 12, 18

Rappahannock River 10, 12, 18

runoff 22

salt water 6, 16, 21

shellfish 4, 6, 24

Susquehanna River 4, 10, 14, 18

tourism 12

urban sprawl 24

watershed 6, 7, 8, 10, 11, 12, 14, 20, 27

wetlands 11, 20, 24

wildlife 8, 9, 17, 21

York River 10, 17, 18